Poems
of the
Spirit

McDougal & Associates
Servants of Christ and Stewards of the Mysteries of God

Poems
of the
Spirit

by

Virginia Jones

Published by:

McDougal & Associates
18896 Greenwell Springs Road
Greenwell Springs, Louisiana   70739
www.ThePublishedWord.com

McDougal & Associates is an organization dedicated to the
spreading of the Gospel of Jesus Christ to as many people as
possible in the shortest time possible.

ISBN 978-1-940461-90-6

Printed on demand in the US, the UK, and Australia
For Worldwide Distribution

Dedication

This book of Spirit-inspired poems is dedicated:

First and foremost, to Jesus and to the working of His Holy Spirit in my life. He has never left me without a thought to write down on paper, whether it was a message, a song or a poem. Just as He spoke to John the Revelator and said, *"Write in a book, and send it unto the seven churches which are in Asia"* (Revelation 1:11), the Holy Spirit is still reminding men and women everywhere to keep a record of all that He has to say and to then pass it on to others. I am determined to do my part as the Spirit anoints me.

To my husband, Howard, the love of my life, who has been an inspiration to me through thick and thin and who encourages me to explore new horizons,

To my children, Stephanie and her husband Kevin, Curtis and his wife Jennifer, Christopher and Mathew, who all hold my heart.

To my eight brothers and sisters whom I love and adore.

Last, but never least, to my church family. You bless me beyond measure.

Acknowledgments

I want to acknowledge the Lord, of course, Who is the center of all my thoughts that are ultimately written down. It has been His Holy Spirit Who has taken me on the journey of life through the study of His Word, waking me up many times at night and placing one word in my spirit and directing me to get up and study it until I have found the truth that He wants to share with me. His love and kindness has brought me through many storms in life and has always landed me safely on the other side of that lesson with the understanding that He is so very faithful to me. His Word has truly been a light unto my feet and a lamp unto my path (see Psalm 119:105).

I also want to acknowledge Harold and Andrea "Andy" McDougal for the time and effort they have taken to read over and prepare this book for publication. Their patience and kindness to me has been such a blessing. I consider them to be a mighty man and woman of God.

I want to acknowledge my family: my hubby of forty-six years and my pastor, Howard, my four children—Stephanie and her husband Kevin, Curtis and his wife Jennifer, Christopher and Mathew—our grandchildren and great-grandchildren who have provided us much infectious laughter and been the subject of many of the poems I have written down through the years. Their joy has always been my inspiration, and their love is the glue that keeps me together.

It is with pleasure that I acknowledge my church family who support me in my efforts to launch out into the depths of wherever the Lord leads my footsteps.

I acknowledge my siblings who have shared the hard times as well and the good times, teaching us all to trust the Lord.

Contents

Introduction

I was born into a family of eight siblings. Mother was a homemaker, and Dad was a sawmiller. Times were hard in southeast Oklahoma, but we never went hungry or had a lack of love in our home.

Dad was a hard-working and God-fearing man. Although he didn't always "have it all together," he made sure he kept his family from going hungry.

Mother made up for any lack we may have felt, either of love or of material goods. She was quite a seamstress and made many of our clothes from flour sacks or hand-me-downs. But her greatest accomplishment in our lives was in making sure we knew about Jesus. She would gather us all in the living room every evening and read the Bible to us, and then we would all kneel and pray together.

Mother had great faith for her children to be saved, and church was both our spiritual and social life up into our teenage years. As I was writing this, I realized that we are all serving the Lord, four as ministers or ministers of music. Two of our siblings have already gone to be with the Lord, as have both of our parents. So there are just six of us left.

As I look back on my childhood, I realize that my whole life has been a rhyme of some sort. From my very early days, I was accustomed to taking long walks and having long talks with God, and I have always felt that He was the reason words came to me so easily and putting them together as I received them just seemed to be the way they should go—rhyme upon rhyme. It was always a wonderful way to pass the time, share a story or give the gift of love.

As I grew up, I remember making up little poems about anything and everything in life. I actually began writing poems down as a means of passing the time in the last hour of a daily literature class when I was in the seventh grade. I shared this custom with a close friend and classmate named Gloria. She and I enjoyed the last hour of each day together. One of us would write the first sentence of a poem, and the other would have to come up with the next sentence that rhymed. This would continue until we were satisfied that the poem was finished. Because of this custom, the school year seemed to end all too soon.

Then, again, at the age of sixteen, I began to compose poems, as the Spirit would inspire me, and I wrote many of them down in the coming years. Then, in 2013, the Holy Spirit really began to draw me into an urgency to write about life in general, life in the Word and life in Christ Jesus.

After my husband came home from a missionary trip to Africa, he came in one day and said to me, "Virginia, I believe you need to gather your poems and put them in a book." My spirit bore witness with this project and, as you can see, my recent poems are now in a book that I can share with you. I hope you enjoy reading them as much as I enjoyed writing them. These *Poems of the Spirit* are about life—past, present and future.

Virginia Jones

Thou wilt shew me
the path of life: in thy
presence is fulness of joy;
at thy right hand there are
pleasures for evermore.
— Psalm 16:11 —

Poems of the Spirit

Poems of the Spirit will help you see
It's all about life, for you and for me.
Whether in the dessert or in a raging storm
Read it with a knowing,
That life is just the norm.
We all have some good days
And, yes, some bad ones too.
But it's when we look
Through the Spirit's eyes,
Troubles seem so very few.
Take heart, my friends,
And you will see,
Jesus can be found in a poem,
Loving you and me!

A Trucker's Life [1]

The life of a trucker has its charm
From open roads to quaint little farms.
Border towns I see in view,
Wishing I was home, sharing with you.

Diesel rigs on left and right,
What a convoy I have in sight,
Making their way to Mexico!
But I'm holding my own on this old road.

The sound of the engine purrs real sweet
While I'm bouncing around in this big old
seat.
I'll hammer down or I'll go real slow.
Just don't send me back to Mexico.

Kansas farms make my eyes itch.
They burn so bad I nearly hit the ditch.
The life of a trucker ... it's in my blood.
But sometimes I wish, yes, I wish I could
Stop all this running and rambling too,
And get me a job selling flat-toed shoes.

---

1. Written in 2013

Change [2]

Change is going to happen.
This is plainly clear.
From the changing of the time
To the friends we hold so dear.
We should never get accustomed
To the plans that we have made
Cause life is sure to change 'em
Even those in marble we have laid.

Change can make us happy
Or make us weep in tears.
It can keep us pressing forward,
Even in the midst of fears.
Change has no boundaries,
No chains to hold us down.
Cause when the time comes for moving,
All barriers are let down.

Change will keep us going
Toward the future. This is true.
And change will never present itself
With a rear-view mirror to view.

---

2. Written in 2015

So, keep your chin up, Sunny.
Don't get the changing blues.
Just saddle up your pony
And put on those ever-changing shoes.

My Mission Vision

Now here's a little story
That may seem unreal
To the unbeliever
Or the run of the mill.
But I tell you no lie.
This is how it came to be.

While praying one day
Upon my knees,
A heavenly vision
Came into view.
The face of a youngster
In a nice new suit,
Golden-blond hair
And a round sunny face.

Then I had an impression of missions,
So I embraced
To pray in the Spirit
For quite some time,
Not knowing this man
Would ever I find.

Many years passed.
It seemed quite a few.
But I kept this vision
Always in my view,
Not really knowing why
Or if it was to be.
Just trusting in the Lord
Who holds the eternal key

But God does all things well,
As you can plainly see.
For one day, in my path,
This plan came to be.
A young man came to town,
To preach his heart's delight,
At Sister Ann's church.
My joy was out of sight.

Little did I realize
Right before my eyes,
Was the man
Who had God's attention.
But I was none the wise.
For you see,

Time had changed him.
"No longer just a lad,"
The Holy Spirit said.
"This is he,"
But I could not be had.
I mused within my spirit
"How could this thing be?"
For it had been so long ago
Praying on my knees.
Little did he realize
What he was about to do,
When he held up the missions card
And trusted what God would do.
For, you see, this was my answer,
As I warred within myself,
"Is this he? Or is this me,
Talking to myself?"

That's when the Lord spoke clearly
What I was supposed to do,
Step out in the aisle,
Myself to him I must introduce.

So quickly I stepped out
Before I lost my nerve,
Hoping he would not think me strange
And praying for the right words.

His kindness was abundant,
This was plain to see.
I finally had a name to the vision
That God had given me.

So, if you are wondering
Just what that name might be,
Let me introduce you
To this man called Apostle Jeremy.
So, I thought it was complete,
Just to meet the man
Who had God's attention
About an eternal plan.
But that was only the beginning,
Now I plainly see,
For he has blessed us abundantly
With a great big family. [3]

---

3. I waited more than thirty years to write this poem about a vision I
   had in 1986. The Lord brought it full circle when He introduced
   us to Apostle Jeremy LaBorde in 2015. God never starts anything
   in us that He will not complete. Thank You, Jesus, for Your
   goodness and mercy.

Step by Step [4]

When my steps are weary
And I don't know where to go,
I set my face toward Jesus,
Blessed Anchor of my Soul.

He hold me in His mercy,
His grace abounds much more
Though the storms, they are raging
And the tempest beats me sore.

I walk toward the goodness
Of Love's enduring grace.
He puts His arms about me
And hides me in His brace.

The steps of a good man
Are ordered by the Lord.
The fool may wander from Him,
But He is my Reward.

---

4. Written March 14, 2015

And though I walk on water
Or the burning sand,
I have faith just in knowing
He will always hold my hand.

Words [5]

I find words are my best friends
When I take them out and put them in again.
Words are, without a doubt,
Funny and amusing
And sometimes quite confusing.

Words can hurt, and words can heal.
Words can be desperate or words can chill.
I play with them from day to day.
I shorten them, so they will stay.
I stretch them out, if you get my drift,
And give them volume,
So, through time, they will sift.

But the greatest words that I have found
Are in God's Word,
Now that book's sound.
Those words give direction and caution, too,
Or give you judgment, when wrong you do.
Christ's words give peace and serenity.
Find His words of love,
And you have found the key.

---

5. Written April 9, 2015

Now I know I sound a little wordy,
But don't you think it's "purdy."
Cause beauty is fainting.
Its only skin deep.
But words last forever,
And from them you will reap.

Measuring Time

How do you measure your time?
Is it measured in length or in rhyme?
Can you spend it like a dime?
Tell me, my friend,
How do you measure time?

Is it the length of your day,
Or the time you counted
All the things you had to say?
Is it measured in months
Or in days or in years?
Or is it a ruler that measures all your fears?
Do you go to great lengths
To account for the time
You live out your life
With some peace of mind?

Does time run away, when life's in a tizzy?
Or does it go slow,
When your really, really busy?
Moments can turn to hours
And hours into days.

But life can't be measured
In any of these ways.

The time you spend down here, my friend,
Is never wasted if you're born again.
So, keep your time bottled on a shelf
And enjoy each day,
As if it's the only one left.
And watch your time reproduce itself.
As it blesses you with perfect health.

The Color of Red [6]

There are many colors in the rainbow,
Red, purple, blue and green.
But the color that
Means the most to me
Washed every sin and stain.

There's much to be said
About the color scheme.
But the life's blood Jesus shed
When He died upon the tree
Holds such a deep meaning
To the heart, who is always leaning
On the One Who came to set us free.

R stands for redemption.
He paid that awful cost.
E stands for eternity.
For me this was bought.
D stands for destiny.
He holds mine in His hands.
Yes, red holds the meaning
Of a pure salvation plan.

---

6. Written May 8, 2015

Searching for the Answers

If you're searching for the answers
But always come up short,
Maybe the place you are searching
Doesn't have a door.

If your life is full of questions
And answers very few,
Maybe where you're looking
Doesn't have a view.

If your standing in the midst
Of a very scary time,
Move over and let Jesus
Fill your troubled mind.

Look into the Good Book.
His words they are life
And filled with added meaning
To take away the strife.

It really is no mystery
If we put it in His hands.
Cause He holds all the tomorrows.
Aren't you glad He has a plan?

When Jesus Made Mud Pies and Opened Blinded Eyes [7]

One day, as Jesus was passing by,
He met a man with blinded eyes.
The disciples thought that he had sinned
Or that his parents did offend.
But Jesus said, "Nay," to either word.
It's not this mans fault
Or his parents by birth.
But that God the Father
Would receive praise,
Will I open his eyes.
And all will be amazed.

So He spit on the ground
And made some clay.
Then he rubbed it on his eyes
And sent him away
To a pool called Siloam.
And there he was made clean.

---

7. Based on John 9, this poem was written on May 23, 2015, as the
Spirit gave me the words.

Realizing, for the first time in his life,
That he could see.

The religious crowd was furious.
Who could this man be?
Who dare heal on the Sabbath day?
Or set a blind man free?
So, they asked the man,
"How do you see?"
And the man who had been blind said,
"It was Jesus Who touched me!"
"Where is He," they then all cried,
"That we may know Him.
Where does He abide?"
But the blind man knew not
Where He would be,
So they pressed Him the more
As to why he could see.

His parents were called.
No help were they.
For fear of the crowd,
They could not say
Then again they pressed on the man
Now not blind,

"Who is this Jesus?"
"He's one of a kind.
He's a prophet," said the man
Who now could see.

"Are you looking for Him
Because of what He did for me
You call Him a sinner,
Because He made mud pies
And sent me to wash
And cleanse my blind eyes.
I know not, if He be sinner or saint.
But I do know, I was blind,
And now I ain't!
He opened my eyes that I might see.
And I worshiped Him because I believed."

"Now, I stand as a witness,
The Good Book, it is true.
Because He looked into my heart
And gave me a clear view
Not that I was physically blind
And that I could not see,
But that my heart was clouded,
And sin had a hold on me.

He opened up the eyes of my heart.
And now I clearly see,
That the blood of Jesus has cleansed me.
How could this miracle be?"

So I be like the blind man,
In John chapter 9.
Cause He took the scales from my heart,
Now I'm no longer blind.
I see the path He has for me,
To shake off the old man
And live abundantly.
I see He is the Great I AM,
The risen King to every lamb.

I see He is the Door,
Enticing me to see so much more.
I see He is the Rock of Ages,
From which His love does pour,
Giving me the strength each day,
Just to endure.
I see Him in the storms of life,
Speaking peace to each day
Giving me His precious grace,
To help me along the way.

I see Him coming in the clouds.
Every eye shall behold.
And one day we will see Him face to face,
As time and end unfolds.

Every Little Thing Matters [8]

Every little thing matters
As you go from day to day,
From the smelling of the roses,
To the flowers in early May.
Don't take life for granted.
It soon will pass away.
And you will be left wondering
What happened to the day?

When all the birds were singing
Such a melody,
Crowding out the buzzing
Of the busy bumble bees.
Every little thing matters
To the Father up above,
Who gave us every little thing
To watch and see and love.

Life is swiftly passing by.
It's very plain to see,

---

8. Written May 8, 2015

From winter's end
To spring again,
For all the world to see.

Take notice, O dear heart.
Don't let it slip away.
For the Father's ever watching
Just how we spend our day.
The gift of life is awesome,
From the birth unto the grave,
Of every little creature
And in every little way. [9]

---

9. His eye is on the sparrow, and I know He's watching over me.

Plunging Through

Plunging through the billows
Of life's uncertain task,
I wondered onto something
That will forever last.
I cradled it close to me,
Holding on to it so tight,
Wanting to keep it forever
In dawn's first early light.

My intentions were so worthy,
My thoughts filled with joy.
I had found the only thing
That could make me feel alive.
So I bundled it together
And tied it with a string,
Not wanting for to share it,
This precious little thing.

But salvation is to be shared,
Much to my surprise.
Regardless of how I kept it in,
It always would arise.

---

10. Written May 8, 2015

So I wear it on the outside
It's pretty as can be.
But I keep it on the inside.
Cause thats how Jesus set me free.

Now I'm beaming from the rooftops
And shining all day long,
Cause I don't have to hide it.
Yes, that's my story!
And this is my song!

Taking Care of Business [11]

Life is oh, so busy,
As I go from day to day.
I wonder if I'll ever find
The end of the way.
There are clothes in the washer
And dishes in the sink,
Floors to sweep and lawns to mow.
Oh, man it's been a week!
But life is as a vapor.
The Good Book tells us so.
I may not finish everything.
It's such a heavy load.

But, I know that my Creator
Sees me as I am
And beckons me to come to Him.
He is the great I AM.
So, chores undone,
I have to run
To the arms of my dear Lord,
Where I will find
He is so kind to lift the heavy load

11. Written May 8, 2015

40

And give me strength to carry on
This really busy road.
So, I will walk each step I take
Hand in hand with Him.
I'll take my plight
To walk in the Light
Knowing I can trust the great I AM!

Killing Time [12]

They ask me what I'm doing.
I say, "Just killing time."
Don't really know the meaning.
It's just an empty line.
We use our words so lightly,
As we toss them all around.
Sometimes empty meanings
Can be so profound.
Like ...
"An ounce of prevention
Is worth a pound of cure."
Sounds like something mom would say,
But, in truth, you can endure.
Or ...
"I will catch you later."
It has a catchy tune.
But have you ever seen
Someone catching up with you?
Words are so funny.
I love them just the same.
Cause words can trick your memory
Or make you look so lame.

---

12. Written May 8, 2015

So, be quick to listen and slow to speak.
The Bible tells us so.
Don't let it slip! Just get a grip!
And, for Heaven's sake,
Don't put your mouth on overload.

In Still Waters [13]

I find in still waters
God's mercy truly flows,
Leading me in paths of life,
Where hope seldom grows.
His love can make the dessert green,
Make flowers bloom in spring.
His peace is overwhelming
As the gentle rain.
No greater love could e'er be found,
That pours out like pure gold,
Showering me from head to toe
And lifting my heavy load.
So, in the sweet forever,
I'll be there by and by,
And sing the songs of highest praise
That reach up to the skies.
Till then, I'll tread still waters,
Listening with a sigh,
For the still, small voice inside my heart
Reminds me in Him there is eternal life!

---

13. Written on May 23, 2015

Jesus, My All-In-All [14]

Jesus, is my All-in-All.
He saved me from my downward fall.
When I answered His holy call,
And laid down all my self-righteous law,
He put a hook in my jaw.
When His mercy I plainly saw.
It's not "the luck of a draw."
It's His precious blood, ya'll.

He is my All-in-All.
And on His name I do earnestly call.
Because I know His is my all,
There's no time to step back and stall
Or give the devil his victory ball,
So, testify for Jesus
And kick Satan in the jaw.
And show the world Who is truly
Your All-in-All!

---

14. Written on February 13, 2016

Hope

If you're tired of feeling lonely
And don't know what to do,
Just fix your heart on Jesus.
Cause He can see you through.
Hope has no stopping place.
So, if you think your near the end,
Just put your trust in Jesus
Because on Him we can depend!

Faith

Faith is a melody
That sings its song to me,
Of how God sent His only Son,
That I may be set free.
Faith will overflow
Into your heart each day,
As you look to His holy Word
And take heed to what He has to say.
Faith grows by love
Sent from the Father up above,
And faith holds the key
That unlocks the door for me!

Love

His love is a drenching rain,
Flowing down to make me clean,
Filling me with His mercy,
And showering me just the same.

His love washes me from the inside out,
Teaching me, I too can love,
Using His compassion
From His storehouse up above.

His love flowed so freely
From the cross. He did bleed,
Spilling out His precious blood.
This is the price He paid for me.
How could I not love Him,
For all that He has done?
From the cradle to the cross,
Our God gave His only Son!

The Voice of Dementia ¹⁵

I am the voice of a dreaded disease.
My short-term memory
Makes me forget things.
I still love my family.
My heart they do fill.
But sometimes is seems
That life is not so real.
I am always looking
For a place called HOME,
And for so many loved ones
Who have already gone on.
You may think me crazy
Or a little odd.
But my mind will wander
Until I sleep in the sod.
But deep down within me,
I'll always be me.
And one glorious morning,

---

15. Written in 2016 in memory of my sister Linda. In 2015 she was diagnosed with dementia, and by 2016 she was already in her heavenly home. In the aftermath, I needed to describe what it was like to see someone you dearly loved lose all sanity and live in the confines of such a dreaded disease. Linda inspired me in more ways than she will ever know. I love you, Big Sis. This is for you!

My mind will be free.
So, play with me and dance with me.
Give me kisses until I see your face,
And help me keep my dignity
As I run this lonely race.
Just cry with me when I am sad,
And laugh with me when I am glad.
Cause one day it will be all gone,
As I take my flight to my new Home,
And find those loved one
You could never see,
Even though you tried
Just to be nice to me.
Then we will rejoice
Until you get Home,
Knowing here in Heaven
I am finally HOME!

Mighty God

To God, let everyone give praise.
On the housetop, don't stop!
In Your beauty, I stand amazed!
What a celebration Your love gives every
day.
And I watch You share Your life's love
In so many ways.
The mighty cannot control You.
The wicked cannot stand
In the presence of our risen King,
Who proclaims He's coming again.
Death did not hold Him,
Nor turn His thoughts astray,
As He rose again that third day.
All my hope in Him I lay!

We're Gonna Pass the Test [16]

Were gonna pass the test, my friend.
Were gonna pass the test.
He's the Rock of all the ages.
He's my World, I must confess.
Jesus ... He is my Savior,
And I'm gonna praise His name.
No trouble can overtake me
Cause He's already broken those chains.

— 1 —

O, Satan tries to tempt me
With troubles every day.
He tries to make my burdens heavy,
Sends darts of doubt my way.
But I've put my trust in Jesus,
Blessed Anchor of my soul,
And I'll be shouting, "Hallelujah!"
So just let the glory roll.

---

16. Written on February 3, 2017

— 2 —

My friend, if you're in trouble
And Satan's on your case,
Just have a little talk with Jesus.
He'll help you run this race.
You don't have to worry
Cause Satan hasn't won.
Turn over your troubles to Jesus
Cause 1 John 4:4 is His gun.

— 3 —

Ye are of God, little children,
And you have overcome them.
For greater is He who holds your hand
Than he who rules this land.
Jesus makes your burdens lighter.
He gives joy every day.
And you'll be shouting, "Hallelujah!"
As you go on your way.

Sharing the
Gift of Love [17]

The gift of love
Came down from above
In the form of human flesh,
With tiny toes and a button nose,
And soft little wrinkles and folds.
His mother often pondered within her heart
As she watched her young Son grow,
What would become of Him.
So little and yet so bold!
Life would prove its pressure,
As this child became a man.
Gifts seemed His specialty,
As He roamed from town to town,
Healing the sick and raising the dead.
Such gifts were never known.
Still He was the greatest gift ever sown.
For God so loved the world
That He gave His only begotten Son,
That whosoever believes in Him
Should not perish,
But have everlasting life.
— John 3:16

_____

17. Written in 2017

The Gift [18]

The Gift came wrapped
In swaddling clothes.
'Twas such a sight to see,
As shepherds gathered
Round Him there
So tiny as could be!
Lying in a manger bare,
This Child, so meek and mild,
Would one day be the Savior
Who would have thought it of this Child?
And who could have imagined Him
Raising folks from the dead?
As He cooed and cuddled with Mary dear,
His mother, as the prophets said.
When God came down from deity
Wrapped up in fleshy sod,
Who could have known
The price was sown
When He died there on the cross?
No greater gift e'er given
To all of mortal man,
This precious baby Boy,

---

18. Written November 8, 2017

With power in His hands
To heal the sick,
Raise the dead,
Or set captives free.
What greater gift
Could you receive
In all of humanity?
So, celebrate
And bring good cheer,
So all the world can see
The Child born in Bethlehem
Is the greatest Gift you will ever receive!

Everything Has a Voice [19]

Everything has a voice,
Just as we all have a choice,
From the grasshopper chirp,
To the thunders roll
To the tiny little mouse
Squeaking out its soul.
All God's creation was given a voice,
To speak, to cry, to sing and rejoice.
The hills are not silent,
As they stand alone,
Giving forth sounds
Of creatures they home.
The sea has its billows,
To sound in the night
Bringing seaman home,
As the harbor gives forth light.
The creeks give a trickle
Of sound you can hear
That gives its life
To the rabbit and deer.
The church sounds its bells,
And Lord, do they ring!

---

19. Written October 10, 2017

Sounding out the melody
That ushers in our King.
The children have their laughter.
It sounds so true and clear.
Knowing in their playtime,
They should never have a care.
Trees voice their longing
As they softly sway,
With the wind that whispers
Through their leaves,
Enjoying another day.
Even time, who has no voice,
Seems to always say,
"Hurry up! Hurry up!
Or you will miss some rays."
Then I remember
Of one still voice
That gently leads me on,
Reminding me to take my time
And let this ole world pass on.
Cause life is so fleeting,
We need to do our best
To let her pass peacefully.
Else we might fail the test.
So, in your life of hurry,

As you pass along,
Remember Christ is still the One
Who is leading us along,
His voice gently calling,
To take us safely o'er.
Knowing when we get there,
We will never ever leave that shore.
Softly and tenderly Jesus is calling.
Won't you come on in?
For it's His voice that will
Determine our way,
From beginning to the end.
All of creation has its own voice.
Listen close to hear the distinction
Before you make a choice!

From the Cradle
to the Cross

One dark and starry night,
Much to Mary's hearts delight,
A Child was born,
God's own Son.

What a wonderful heavenly sight!
Little is known of His childhood
Except that He went around doing good.
He taught in the Temple
The stories of old
With amazing authority
And a voice that was bold.

Mary, in her heart did ponder
Just how His life would unfold,
Knowing somehow He would carry
A very heavy load.

Peace on Earth, good will to men!
One day His blood would pardon men's sin.
No greater love has ever been shown.

From the cradle to Calvary,
He went alone!

Death could not hold Him down.
From the cradle to the cross,
That was His victory ground.
As the stone was rolled away,
He walked out of the tomb that day,
Triumphant over death, Hell and the grave.
I am so glad I can say, "My Jesus saves!"

Just Listen

Lately I've been listening
To the news across the land,
How the war on terrorist is rising,
And they say, "It will never end!"
As fear spreads across this country
And folks are in dismay,
I wonder if they ever talk to Jesus
And ask what He would say.

All the money there is in Fort Knox
Cannot save this wearisome land.
For we all know it was founded on
"In God we trust,"
And not the fortunes of man.
Now ISIS is upon us
And our boarders are opened wide,
And only Jesus can save us.
Its in Him we can safely hide.

But Wall Street is too busy
Putting dollars away.
And our tax money is going

To some things that will
Just vanish away.

It's time we put our trust,
In the only One Who cares,
And listen to what He has to say
And realize Jesus will always be there.

Then we will see
A change in this land.
As we humble ourselves in prayer,
God will heal the heart of man.
And His blessings He will share!

My Little Prayer Rock

I have a little prayer rock.
It reminds me to pray.
Each morning, as I look at it,
I remember how to start my day.

I confess my sins to Jesus.
He hears me when I say,
"I'm sorry that I failed You, Lord.
Give me mercy, this I pray."

Then I remembered my neighbor
Whom I spoke so harshly to,
And the little rock reminds me
Confession, though hard,
Will see you through.

My little prayer rock is jagged,
Which tells me life can get rough.
But then I remember this little rock
Is as solid as God's love.

So I keep my little prayer rock
Close to my side each day,
Cause it keeps me ever humble,
And reminds me to confess as I pray.

Don't Shut Me Out [20]

When your heart is heavy in doubt,
Because your soul took a foolish route,
And you hang your head and pout
Over some stupid reason to shout,
If you listen real close, you can hear
The Lord's voice so loud and so clear,
"Don't shut Me out!"

Even if you are not on the right route,
Just turn your heart about.
"Give heed to My voice," our Lord will say.
"Humble yourself and pray.
Don't let fear be your dismay.
Overcome all your doubt.
I'll show you the right route.
And you will be on your way.
To a bright and beautiful day.
Cause love holds no hate,
And it's never too late
To bow your head and pray,
'Lord, teach me never to stray!' "

---

20. Written August 26, 2017

Missing in Action ²¹

My prayer goes out today for the soldiers
Who have fought for this land
And are held captive against their will
And can't come home again!
I pray for God's grace to see them
through,
Till he brings their deliverance into view!
I also pray for that mother or that dad
Who are missing in action,
Even in our Homeland,
Who laid down the sword
And refused to fight
For their children's well-being
And their God-given rights!
I pray for the missionary on the field
Who lost the vision of what is really real!
I pray for the pastor
Who threw his towel in,
Who thought it was easier
To not preach against sin!
I pray for the singer

---

21. Written June 21, 2017

Who gave up their song
For the fame and the fortune
And a life that's all wrong!

I pray for the ones
Who say they know God
But never go to church
Or tell of His love!
I pray for the person
Sitting on the pew
Who says they know Jesus,
But their actions are few!
So many are missing in actions, it seems.
Where are all the seekers
Who once had a dream?
Shouldn't we shake ourselves
To see if we are the ones
Missing in action today?

Amen!

The Prodigals [22]

There was a certain man
Who had two sons.
The elder was committed,
But not the younger one.

In fact, the younger said,
"Ole man, give me all that's mine,
Cause, I believe it's time
To take in the re-fine,
To explore the great unknown.
There are seeds to be sown.
Yes, I believe that I am now grown."

The father completed the task,
Dividing his goods as was asked.
To each son he gave his living,
Not even holding back in his giving.
What compassion this father did have,
To show such love to each lad!

The elder stayed on as before.
The younger soon hit the door,

---

22. Written November 26, 2017

Making his way, his money soon spent,
With riotous living. His pride was intent.

But just as the father did feel,
The younger son soon would appeal,
For he found himself down on his luck,
Wallowing in a pig pen
Of the worries of muck.
He came to himself, in his agony,
Hoping for a servant's job.
At least he would be home,
Safe and sound.
Cause this ole world had let him down.

But little did he realize
His father would soon visualize,
And come running to meet him there
In that place of great despair,
With a robe, a ring and shoes for his feet,
And make for him a fatted calf to eat.
And party they would,
Till their heart's content.
The son had come home.
How much it had meant!

The father called for the elder to enter in,
But the music and laughter soon did offend.
For the elder felt he was being left out.
"Why did the father bring this all about,
For a greedy little boy
Who thought he could win
At the game of chance."
Just look where he's been!

But the father, in his loving way.
Told the elder, "I'm so glad that you stayed.
For all I have has been yours all along.
Come, join our singing,
This welcome-home song."
For some will go, and some will stay,
But it's in the Father's hand His will to obey.
Forgiven little, forgiven much,
Still we all need the great Father's touch.
Let this poem be a reminder too.
Regardless of the sin, many or few,
No one goes unnoticed
By the Father's glance.
So, sing the songs of Zion,
And bring on, Victory, your dance!

The Sower [23]

Behold a sower went out to sow.
Some seeds fell to the wayside,
Don't you know.
Birds came and devoured every one of
them,
Meaning, we must hold on
To Gods Word from within!

Some seeds fell on stony ground,
But when it grew up,
No ground was found.
Then the hot sun quickly cut it down,
Cause God's Word needs faith to abound.

Some of the seed fell among the thorns,
But words of life are never forlorn.
Life and death cannot co-exist.
And if we chose death,
We won't make Heaven's list.

---

23. Based on Matthew 13, this poem was written November25, 2017.

Sow His seed into good ground,
And watch God's blessings tenfold
abound.
As good fruit springs forth from within,
Some a hundred, some sixty,
And some thirty, my friend.

Goodbye to 2017 [24]

2017 is about to give its final ring.
As they drop the ball in the square,
Shouts will be heard from everywhere.

Another year gone by, yes, it's true.
What did it change for me and you?
Did you count each day
A blessing, my friend?
Or did you dread each day
From beginning to end?

Did each day bring
A cup of good cheer,
Giving thanks to the Father
Who held you so dear?
Did you ponder His goodness
In each passing day,
Knowing without Him
You would've lost your way?

---

24. Written December 30, 2017

For He is Hope for tomorrow,
Sharing His mercy and grace.
His love is overflowing,
As you go on your way.
Did you stop to remember
His Word, my friend,
As you toiled each day
From beginning to end?
Was your love His,
Shinning out from within?
When you met the beggar
On the street,
Did it remind you to lend a hand?

Were your days filled with a longing
To grow closer to your Lord,
To open His Word, which is your Sword?
Or did you squander your time,
Wishing life was better too,
Thinking everyone around
Was more blessed than you?

These things I do ponder
As the year closes to an end,
Knowing 2018 is soon to begin.

So, if you missed out
On the blessings this year,
It's never to late to drink
From the Lord's cup of cheer!

At an altar of thanksgiving,
Yes, that's where it begins.
So, gird up your loins
And let the New Year ring in,
With glory and honor
To the risen King,
As we sing "Hallelujah in 2018"!

We serve a risen Savior
For each and every year.
He holds us in the presence,
As He dries our every tear.
"May the Lord richly bless you"
Is my prayer!

This Joy that I Have ²⁵

Jesus said, "I am the Vine.
Trust in Me,
If you are Mine,
You're the branches
Sprung out from Me
Bringing forth good fruit
For all the world to see.
Push it forth and let it grow,
So everyone will see and know,
That I'm in you,
And you're in Me,
Fit for the Kingdom,
A strong, steady tree!

But, for the branches who
Refuse to grow
Or bring forth fruit
For the world to know,
Will be cut off from the Vine within,
Because they fashioned their life
After a world of sin.
For without Me, you cannot be
Flowing in the Spirit of my mercy tree
There will be no fruit for you to bear.

25. Written December 13, 2017

For I have severed all fruit from
Your world of care.
The choice is yours. Can't you see?
If you abide in Me, I will abide in thee.
Ask what you will, and it shall be done,
Through God the Father,
God the Spirit
And Jesus, the only begotten Son.

So, give glory to the Father,
Through the Spirit of the Son,
Who lives in us and abides in us
Until this race is run.
If we keep His commandments
And walk in His will,
His joy will remain
Till we are all completely filled.

I HAVE NO GREATER JOY THAN TO HEAR
THAT MY CHILDREN WALK IN TRUTH.
3 JOHN 1:4

Blessed Be His Name [26]

Woke up to this,
Sung by a choir of black people,
With a full orchestra:

Blessed be His name!
Blessed be His name!
Blessed be the name
Who heals the sick and lame!

Blessed be His name!
Blessed be His name!
Blessed be the name
Who brings victory to man!

Blessed be His name!
Blessed be His name!
Blessed be the name
of our Lord!

Oh, I will
Bless His holy name!
I bless His holy name!

---

26. Written April 30, 2017 as seen in a vision.

I will bless the holy name of my Lord!
Bless His holy name!
Bless His holy name!
I will bless the holy name of our Lord!

I Know a Man [27]

I know a Man
With scars in His hands,
A Man whose love
Is a sweet as a Dove,
A Man who bled
And died for me
Upon a cross
Called Mt. Calvary.
If you don't know this Man
I'm talking about,
Then, within your heart,
Don't doubt,
He can cleanse you
And make you whole,
Remove all burdens,
For He love you so.
Give Him a chance
To show you how
To live this life
Without a doubt.
And hold Him dear,
Within your heart,
For He is a Friend
That never will depart!

27. Originally written in 1973, this poem was rewritten in 2018.

Read It Till You Breathe It [28]

Read It till you breathe It.
Let God's Word sink in.
Read It till you breathe It.
Then read It once again.
It's healing for your body
And refuge for your soul.
Read it in the midnight
Till the fragrance takes control.
It has a destination,
To fortify within,
And build up your inner man.
Read It, my child, again!

---

28. Based on Ephesians 6:3, this was written on April 21, 2018.

Keeping the Faith

Keep the faith
With His grace.
Win the war
Before doubt deplores.
Don't look back
You'll get off track.
Keep the faith
By mercy and grace.
Don't give in
To fear and sin.
Keep the faith.
We win in the end.
Don't let faith
Take a bend.
Keep it strong.
Don't give in.
Keep the faith, my friend.
God gave you a measure
To live in Him!

---

29. Written on April 14, 2018.

Garden of Grace, Seeds of Faith [30]

In my garden of grace,
The Lord has given seed
For me to place.
I dare not put it in rocky ground,
Else my plants will not abound.
I dare not put it in soil untended,
Or my seeds will be bird offended.
For they will eat my seeds, you see,
If the seed has no ground indeed.
So, teach me, Lord, to till the ground
And allow the seed to abound,
That I may share some seed with You,
And bless our Lord. This is what I can do.
I'll till my heart with God's goodness and grace
And allow Him to remove all roots in place
So that the seeds that I sow
Will spring forth, all in a row.
Some thirty, some sixty or one hundred be.
Yes, that's God's seed
Working mightily in me!

---

30. Written on February 23, 2018

On Ephesians 4

1. If you a prisoner be,
Walk worthy of the Lord in thee,
Wherewith He has called.
The vocation you have within
Is to come out from evil
And learn to live in Him!

2. With lowliness and meekness of heart,
Give life a brand new start.
With longsuffering forbear.
His love is always there,
To show others how much you care!

3. Endeavor always to keep
Unity in the Spirit of peace!

4. In one body and one Spirit, you're
called.
In hope, Christ paid it all!

5. One Lord, one faith, one baptism.
Yes, Christ Jesus, He is risen!

6. One God and Father of all,
Who is above all and through all
And in you all!

7. But grace was given to every man
By the measure of the gift
Christ has in hand!

8. Wherefore, he ascended way up high,
Setting the captives free. This is no lie.
And gifts He gave to men
Who knew no freedom
From this world of sin!

9-10. Now He ascended above and below
To fill all things in this world of woe!

11. Some He gave apostles,
To build the Church.
And some He gave prophets
To speak His Word.
And some evangelist. Yes, this is true.
To bring in the harvest, no, not a few.
Some he gave pastors
To tend the sheep.
And some He gave teachers
To sow out the seed!

12.To bring us all into
The unity of the faith
To show us He loves us
And reminds us of His grace!

13.Until we all come
To the knowledge and stand

13. In the fulness of His Word,
In the stature of this Man,

13. The Man Christ Jesus.
Yes, that is our goal,
To walk in His fullness ever so bold!

14.Henceforth we walk
Not as children, know ye,
Tossed up and thrown by the wind.
Don't you see?
And carried about
By crafty men to deceive.
"No," my friend, this cannot be!

15. But, speaking truth in love, this we do:
Till Christ is in our head
And our hopes are renewed!

16.From the whole Body
This may we be
Fitly joined together
For all the world to see!
According to the effectual working
Of His master plan,
Making increase of the Body.
Only though His love we can.
Standing in His goodness
And led by God's hand!

17. This I say and testify,
"Don't walk like Gentiles."
In anger and strife,
Puffed up in mind.
They are not kind.
Walk as the Lord
This is a good find!

18. They have no understanding
With darkness of heart
And alienate themselves
Right from the start.
Through ignorance and blindness,
They stumble along,
Never finding peace
And never righting this wrong!

19. A seared-over conscience
With evil in view,
They plan out their uncleanness,
Their greediness to pursue!

20. But you, my friends,
Who trust in Christ,

21. If so be ye have heard Him,
He will tell you no lie!

22. Put off the old man
In conversation and deeds not right,
Which is corrupt, according to deceitful lust.
"Yes, put them all out of sight!

23. And be renewed
In the spirit of your mind.
Jesus paid the cost to keep us in line!

24. Put on the new man and walk after
God
In righteousness and true holiness,
And lay down the old sod!

25. By putting away lying,
Speak truth to every man.

And share a little kindness
Across this great big land.
For we are members of one another,
And walking with Jesus is the key.
So gird up your loins
And let your spirit be free!

26.Even if you get angry,
Don't commit sin.
Give it all to Jesus,
And keep it real, my friend.
Don't go to sleep angry and tired,
For sleep won't come if your mind is mired!

27.Neither give the devil
A place to stay,
Or he will move right in.
And rent he won't pay!

28. Let him that stole steal no more.
Kick him out, and show him the door.
But rather be you working with your hands
Than listening to the devil
Who is making bad plans.
For it's a good thing to work

In a labor of love,
So you can bless someone else
Who's in need of!

29. And keep your conversation
To the goodness of the Lord,
Edifying others
With grace all the more!

30. Grieve not the Holy Spirit,
For it's His joy indeed
To seal you to the Day of Redemption
And fill your every need!

31. So, let all bitterness, wrath and anger
Be put away from you.
It's up to you, my friend,
Which way you will choose.
Don't clamor out loud
Or speak evil, my friend.
Jesus has the answer.
On Him you can depend!

32. Be kind one to another,
Tender hearted as can be,
Forgiving one another.
This is Christlike. Can't you see?

For God showed the example
When He forgave you, my friend,
Sending His Son Jesus,
To free all of us from sin!

The Multitude of Hungry Folks [31]

In a land far away,
Back in the New Testament days,
A multitude came
To see what Jesus had to say.
His teaching was good
And full of truth.
He blessed them there
With more than just food!

As they tarried three days,
The Lord was concerned.
No food had they eaten,
As they sat there to learn!

Compassion had He
To feed each one,
So He asked His disciples,
"Did you bring any buns?"

"No," they cried,
"Where would it be

---

31. Based on Mark 8, this was written on January 8, 2018.

In this wilderness here
As far as you can see?"

So, He asked one of them,
"How many loaves have ye?"
"Seven," they said,
"But how many can that feed?"

He commanded the people
To sit down on the ground.
As He break the loaves,
The disciples gathered round
And took of the bread
To give to the crowd.
Then Jesus broke a few fishes.
A miracle no doubt!

When four thousand people
Got up to go,
No one left hungry,
Not a single soul!

Why, even to-go bags
Were taken up that day,
Seven baskets of mercy,
As He sent them on their way!

That's a big ole miracle
In the making, my friend.
When you spend time with Jesus,
He will fill you to the brim!

Fathers

Fathers are forever,
Or so it should seem.
They hold a special place
In the heart of every dream.
There are big ones and tall ones
And skinny ones too.
They love to make you giggle
When they are playing with you.
Fathers should bring up their children
In the way that they should go,
With love and compassion and honesty
That only a father can know.
They love to take you fishing
Or spend the day skipping rocks
Or take you to the ballpark
And spend their money on lollipops.
Makes no difference how you spend it
When its just the two of you.
Cause fathers who really are fathers
Just want to spend time with you!

Moms [32]

Moms love their children.
This, we all know.
They cuddle them
And keep them from harm,
And so proud, to see them grow.
No greater joy can any mom see
Than to know her children care
That she would give her life for them
And shield them from all fear.
Tears of joy roll down her cheeks
When her babies become women and men.
Cause she knows that she has done her best,
And it's time for them to begin
To live the life instilled in them
Of God's love, mercy and grace,
And set their minds to follow Jesus
Because through Him Each trial they can face.
No greater love could any child know
Than the love a mother gives.
So, remember your mom on Mother's Day
Even if Heaven is now where she lives!

---

32. Written for Mother's Day, May 10, 2015.

He Snores; She Snores [33]

As I lay me down to sleep,
Head on my pillow,
Blanket on my feet,
I hear a noise,
Much to my surprise.
Was it a horse?
Or a tractor?
Or fifty houseflies?

What a bang! What a clamor!
Or a drippy faucet, I bet.
No! I believe it's a flock of geese
Traveling to the south on a jet.

What could this be?
I pondered through the night,
When out came a burr of shivering fright.
The thing that I dreaded
Was the thing I did hear.
The man lying beside me
Was snoring with cheer.

33. Written on December 16, 2017

With a hoot and a howl,
Yes, just as I feared,
My hubby was snoring out a ballad.
OH, DEAR!

Not a symphony or
A good ole Gospel song.
But the ballad I heard
Was noisy and long.
His nariz inflated,
He went on and on,
As he snorted out
"She's done me all wrong!"

Then came the part
Where he took a deep breath.
And, Oh, my Jesus,
I need some rest.
For the next few lyrics
Were too jumbled to tell
If he was singing a song
Or preaching about missing Hell.

As he ended his ballad,
I fell asleep,

Knowing, in the morning,
His secret I would keep.
Understanding full well
It would be my turn tonight,
To snore out some folk song,
To my heart's delight!

Virus [34]

V stands for Victory.
   I will overcome.
I stands for Icky.
   My whole body's on the run.
R stands for Restroom.
   It's become my best friend.
U stands for Until that day
   I feel like a person again.
S stands for Sickness.
   I hate it to the core.

But I'm thankful it's just a **VIRUS**
And will soon walk out my door!

---

34. Written February 9, 2015

Catching Fish [35]

FOLLOW ME AND I WILL MAKE YOU
FISHERS OF MEN. — JESUS

There's this lady I know,
Who lives with a fishing pole,
On the side of the bank
Of the old river called Yank,
Just waiting for someone
To say she can go.

The winter's been long,
And she's had no sun,
But is looking forward to the day
When all her nurses will be gone,
And out to that boat she will run,
Knowing that it won't take long,
For her to catch another big one.

So I bid you adieu,
As you head to the slu,
And may your fishing days
Be filled with fish not a few,

---

35. Written for my friend Norma on her birthday, February 10, 2015.

Giving you lots of memories to view.
May all your fishing dreams come true,
Filled with green onions, taters
And a catfish too.
Its been fun sharing stories with you!

A Better Man [36]

I want to be a better man,
One who knows how to get ahead.
Pursuing life is my big plan.
Giving it my all, yes, I can.
Not fearing what the future holds,
Just knowing I will be as bold
As a roaring lion
That's on the prowl
Or soaring like an eagle
In the great here and now!

Yes, that's my plan,
To be the man
Who walks in truth
And know where I stand.
Cause Momma's prayers
Won't let me down
Nor the Word of God
That I have found.
So I stand in awe
Of the risen King
And thank Him for
The strength to just be me,
A better man!

---

36. Written for Joshua Watts, December 9, 2017

Working for a Living [37]

When your working for a living,
You can plainly see
The days will turn to months
And faded memories.
Cause working for a living
Runs together so,
Your Friday feels like Monday,
And off to work you go.

Working for a living ...
Well, it's plain to see,
It's all about the job, boys.
I'm sure you will agree.
So, if your working for a living,
Hold your head up high.
Cause there's work out there to do, folks.
I bid you all goodbye!

---

37. Written May 8, 21015

Prayers for Jennifer

I woke up this morning,
With news I did fear.
A prayer request was posted
For a needed care.
A dear friend in trouble,
Whose been faithful and true
To the Master in Heaven,
Her sorrows not a few.
I searched in my heart
For the right words to say,
Something that would bless her
And make her hurts go away.

But words cannot always
Be the healing stream.
Sometimes it's the listening
That has a better ring.
You see, life is so uncertain,
And words fall to the ground.
But when you listen from the heart,
Love makes a better sound.

So, dear friend, if you are listening,
And I know that you are,
I am sending prayers to Heaven
From the bottom of my heart!

Whose Report Do You Believe? [38]

Whose report do you believe?
Whose arm will you receive?
Just a tender plant from Bethlehem,
Born in a manger, this Baby Lamb.
His roots of no importance lay.
His Kingdom was not from here, they say.
No form or comeliness would aspire,
Or His beauty to desire.
Despised and rejected,
His sorrows not a few,
Acquainted with grief,
No one would pursue.
Yet He was wounded for my transgression.
That is why I make Him my confession.
He was bruised for my iniquities.
I give Him my heart
And He does please.
The chastisement for my peace
Was upon Him.

---

38. Based on Isaiah 53:1-6, this was written on April 21, 2018.

He did not come here to condemn.
Yes, with His stripes I am healed.
And by His Spirit, I am filled.
All His sheep did go astray,
Everyone to their own way.
Still, He bore our iniquity
When He shed His lifeblood
Upon that tree.
No greater love than this, my friend,
When He bore the price
For all man's sin!

I Bow My Knees [39]

FOR THIS CAUSE I BOW MY KNEES.
Ephesians 3:14-21

For this cause, I bow my knees.
No greater cause than God's love for me.
Yes, for us all, His love proclaims.
According to the richness
Of His amazing grace.
Strengthened with might
In the inner man,
I walk in victory o'er this land.
For Christ does dwell within me.
Rooted and grounded in faith I be,
Comprehending with all the saints
His depth of love. I will not faint
Till I am filled with all of Him
Throughout all the ages
World without end. Amen!

---

39. Based on Ephesians 3:14-21, this was written April 21, 2018.

Andy, Woman of God [40]

I met this lady called Andy,
Cute and spunky and really quite dandy.
Bright was her continence
You could see,
Her face glowing with God's glory.
Chosen of God to be
A powerhouse saint for all to see,
Winning each battle with great victory.
Anointed with a spiritual kind of grace,
Even in danger, she's run the race.
She's quite a perfection all rolled into one.
Cause Jesus lives in her, she's already won.

So, keep the faith, dear friend of mine.
Your words of wisdom will keep us in line
And pave the way for all to see
Faith holds the key for each victory!

I call you BLESSED!

---

40. Written for Prophetess Andy McDougal, April 21, 2018.

Author Contact Page

You may contact Virginia Jones in the following ways:

Email: jones.virgina@yahoo.com

Telephone: 580-212-9456